Ancient Magick for Today's Witch Series

LOVE SPELLS

MONIQUE JOINER SIEDLAK

OSHUN
PUBLICATIONS
oshunpublications.com

Cover Design by MJS

Cover Images by MidJourney

Published by Oshun Publications

www.oshunpublications.com

ANCIENT MAGICK FOR TODAY'S WITCH SERIES

The *Ancient Magick for Today's Witch Series* is a series for modern witches to explore ancient magick, covering Celtic, Gypsy, and Crystal magic, among others. It offers practical advice on spells, rituals, and enchantments for today's use, incorporating natural energies and spiritual connections. With insights into Shamanism, Wicca, and more, it helps readers enhance their magickal journey, offering paths to protection, prosperity, and spiritual growth by combining ancient wisdom with contemporary practice.

Wiccan Basics

Candle Magick

Wiccan Spells

Love Spells

Abundance Spells

Herb Magick

Moon Magick

CONTENTS

INTRODUCTION

We all look for love. You will find useful spells here. Guidance on spell casting and magick, alongside love spells for different types of conditions you may encounter when dealing with love and relationships. Remember, that while a love spell may help you in strengthening your relationship or identifying that someone special, it's not going to do all the work for you. It's not going to impose a relationship where it's not meant to be. What we think we demand, and what our soul essentially needs, sometimes are two different things. Your Spirit will give your soul what it needs to grow and flourish, even if it is a painful experience for you.

Using a love spell to compel someone else to love you will not have you want you in the long run want, which is true love. I feel it's best to do a spell that will lead you the individual that's appropriate for you, not the one person in specific that you appear to be infatuated with. No matter how often you think that the relationship is meant to be, hold it in context and recognize that if it were actually meant to be, you wouldn't have to push it to happen. It will happen when it happen.

Whether or not magick works for you will depend on your mood more than all else. For your spell to be successful, it's vital that you have a confident attitude towards accomplishing your goal. Perform the spells for objectives that you believe are reachable. Magick doesn't work the way you view on TV. Snap your fingers and poof. Magick is a just tool. It's comparable to prayer or creative visualization. Magick assists you to focus your energy and objective so that you're more prone to achieve your goals.

No amount of free powerful love spells, candle love spells, in general love spells, or magick love spells can guarantee you the success at winning your heart's desires, nevertheless it is essential when dealing with affairs of the heart and feelings too:

Be grateful for the coming and/or reappearance of love into your existence.

With love comes accountability. You are responsible for individuals you love as well as who love you, never control or play power or head games.

Take every chance to express your love. Remember the little things. You never know how long for you are going to be in their life, and they in yours. Be yourself. You deserve love like anyone else.

The most important thing to always consider: Be aware of the threefold law with this kind of spell.

Before you begin any spell, remember to have your spell ready ahead of time with all the ingredients. Be certain of the Moon's phase. Be sure that you won't be interrupted since your spell needs to be planned out in advance so that it goes smoothly. Have it planned right down to the time of day and record it into your book of shadows or whatever you are using. If your spell goes well, you might want to do it again. If it fails, then you can tweak it to get better results.

One of the best ways to learn to visualize effectively is to look at something. An apple, your hand, or a photo, anything that will hold still for a while. Really see it. Close your eyes and try to see it in your mind's eye. Right down to the last detail. Then open your eyes to see how close you actually came. After a bit of practice you will be able to visualize in great detail. Visualization is very important with magick.

A Final Thought

Okay, all the love spells in this are probably for beginners. If they work for you and you've find love, I'm happy for you. Love is easy. Everyone wants it. Every boy and every girl.

Mojo)o(

1

CASTING A LOVE SPELL

One of the elements that usually attract new individuals to Wicca as well as other Pagan religions is Love spells. There's a number of debate inside the Pagan community about the integrities of casting a love spell on someone. I mean, if you're performing magick on someone without their awareness, aren't you interfering with their free will?

Many Pagans will advise you that the best course to address love magick is to avoid fixating on a definite individual as an objective.

As a replacement, apply your energy and abilities to focus on yourself. Draw love to you, show yourself as an individual that is deserved of love. You could work your magickal abilities to appear more positive and inviting, like a magickal makeover. Basically, adjust yourself, not someone else. Get someone to see you and later after getting the individual to, once they've spotted you, identify all the details about you that they like.

Bear in mind that plenty of Pagan traditions which have no constraints on the use of magick to transform someone else. If you're part of such a belief, the service of love magick may easily be within the bounds of your ethical guidelines. In some customs of folk magick, love magick is completely acceptable. It's something that's given as a means of course and is no more wrong than putting on a seductive perfume or a sexy push-up bra.

Magick is regarded as an accessory, and can be utilized in tandem with everyday life to bring you what you require -- after all, if you didn't need to change situations, you wouldn't be doing magick in the first place.

Before casting any type of working that influences another individual, though, be certain to consider repercussions. How will your actions affect not simply you, but other individuals? Will it ultimately cause damage?

Will it cause someone to be harmed, either openly or indirectly? These are all factors that should be assessed before executing any working at all, whether it's a love spell or some other type of magick. If your tradition or belief system prevents you from performing magick on someone without their consent or knowledge, then you'd be better off passing up the love magick and focusing instead on self-improvement and self-empowerment.

If you keep this mindset, you should be able to perform love magick and still perform within your ethical bounds.

Knowing how to cast love spells can be half the battle in getting that new romance going in your life. Just having lots of great love spells is only the first step and you can discover some further general techniques on how to cast a spell elsewhere. Right now, it's clearly about that love magick.

Your Aim or Objective

The biggest part of knowing how to cast love spells. Are you casting a spell aimed at a precise individual to alter their feelings, or do you use a basic attraction spell not focused on anybody in particular?

It really lies on the situation. If you are working on a spell to have someone to notice you, then you're not really controlling their feelings, just practicing some magick to draw that person's attention. There's not anything wrong with. Casting a spell on someone specific to produce emotions that aren't really there? That can be riskier and can be begging for trouble down the road on.

Alternatively, a spell that's just positioning your need for love out there for the Universe to focus on is the more classic approach. You will have a better chance of finding a true love rather than constructing it for yourself.

The Methods

So that's about deciding your method, but what about the real methods in what way to cast the love spell. The items that go into a solid love spell may include:

The color pink, red, or white.

The element of water or air.

Herbs like gardenia, rose, damiana, vanilla, ylang-ylang cloves, mandrake, and vervain.

Stones like amber, ruby, jade, red jasper, and garnet.

Personal items or tag lock of your objective (ex. photo, hair, etc.).

If you can, cast your love spells on a Friday. Friday is dedicated to Venus. During your spell, focus all your thoughts on energies and emotions on your objective, whether it is a distinct person or not.

But if your spell is expected to be open to all but you nevertheless have a certain somebody in mind, then in your best interest, do not to focus any thoughts or energy on that individual. Allow your mind to be open or you risk your energy is going to get wasted. Just because you omit someone's name from your spell doesn't signify it won't turn out heading their way because your mind is steady on them.

These are just a few suggestions to keep in mind the next time you're searching for love with a spell.

2

DRAWING LOVE

Ancient belief systems deeply root the philosophy behind attraction spells, intertwining the spiritual and physical realms. These spells, part of a broader category known as love magic, aim to draw love or enhance one's magnetic allure, tapping into the natural energies of the world and the practitioner's personal aura. Attraction spells are not just mechanisms of wish fulfillment but are based on the principles of intention, resonance, and the law of attraction.

Intention and Willpower

At the core of every spell, including those for attraction, lies the practitioner's intention. This is the focused desire or outcome that the spell caster wishes to manifest. In attraction spells, the intention might be to find a new lover, rekindle a relationship, or increase one's desirability. People often believe that the effectiveness of these spells directly depends on how clear and strong one's intentions are. This principle suggests that the universe responds to human thoughts and emotions. Many modern philosophical and psychological theories also echo this concept.

Resonance and Vibrational Energy

It is believed that everything in the universe vibrates at particular frequencies, and attraction spells operate based on the principle of resonance. People believe these spells work by aligning one's personal vibrational energy with the frequencies that attract love. This could involve using specific herbs, stones, or symbols that correspond to love and beauty within magical practice. By harmonizing one's energy with that of what one wishes to attract, one creates a magnetic pull. This is not dissimilar to tuning a radio to a specific frequency to catch a desired station; in magic, the practitioner tunes their energies to attract particular experiences or people.

The Law of Attraction

Closely linked to the concept of vibrational energies is the law of attraction, a philosophy popularized in the early 20th century but grounded in much older magical and mystical traditions. According to this law, positive or negative thoughts bring positive or negative experiences into one's life. Consequently, people who practice attraction spells perceive them as tools for directing their minds towards positive outcomes, which in turn increases the likelihood of manifesting those outcomes. By performing a ritual, the practitioner is essentially setting an intention and visualizing the desired result, which is supposed to draw that reality towards them.

Ethical Considerations

While the philosophy behind the attraction spells is enchanting, it brings up significant ethical considerations. Most traditions emphasize the importance of not infringing on another's free will. Spells meant to attract a specific person, therefore, are often viewed with caution or outright disapproval within many magical communities. The ethical practitioner of magic is encouraged to focus on spells that enhance their personal attributes or prepare them to attract love naturally, rather than spells that coerce or manipulate.

Psychological Perspectives

From a psychological viewpoint, the practice of casting attraction spells can also be seen as a form of ritualized positive thinking. The rituals involved in spell casting help to reinforce one's goals and can significantly boost one's confidence and self-esteem. This can affect how one is perceived by others. Whether one believes in the mystical aspects of spells, the psychological benefits can be substantial.

The philosophy behind attraction spells is multifaceted, incorporating spiritual and psychological elements. Whether viewed through the lens of ancient wisdom or contemporary psychology, these spells encapsulate the human desire to connect with others and the belief in our ability to shape our own lives through intention and belief.

Drawing Love Spells

Drawing love spells is a powerful tool that empowers individuals to attract the romance they seek. By aligning their energies with the potent force of love, these spells open one's heart and enhance personal magnetism. They create an aura that naturally draws in positive, mutually respectful connections. This process involves intention-setting, visualization, and the use of magical correspondences like herbs, crystals, and candles that symbolize attraction and affection.

Keep in mind that successfully drawing love spells requires more than just the right ingredients and rituals. It also requires personal readiness to give and receive love with authenticity. This means embracing self-love and being open to new experiences, understanding that the energy you put into the spell will shape the love that you attract. Your emotional state and readiness play a significant role in the effectiveness of these spells.

Drawing Love Spells

Drawing love spells is a powerful tool that empowers individuals to attract the romance they seek. By aligning their energies with the potent force of love, these spells open one's heart and enhance personal magnetism. They create an aura that naturally draws in positive, mutually respectful connections. This process involves intention-setting, visualization, and the use of magical correspondences like herbs, crystals, and candles that symbolize attraction and affection.

Keep in mind that successfully drawing love spells requires more than just the right ingredients and rituals. It also requires personal readiness to give and receive love with authenticity. This means embracing self-love and being open to new experiences, understanding that the energy you put into the spell will shape the love that you attract. Your emotional state and readiness play a significant role in the effectiveness of these spells.

Personal Love Enchantment

Cast a focused spell to attract love from a specific person, aligning intentions and energy to enhance your allure ethically and draw them closer.

Items Needed:

- Cauldron or Fire Proof Container
- Paper
- Scissors

- Red marker
- Black marker

Directions:

At nighttime light a small fire in a cauldron or whatever you have available to contain the fire. Cut out a piece of paper that's approximately3x3 inches. Draw a heart on paper and color it with red. While visualizing the person, write their name in the heart. Think of his or her burning with desire for you just like the flames of the fire. Kiss the name on the heart 3 times. Place the paper in the fire while saying these words 3 times.

"A fire that comes from down below,

Bring me my love that I now know.

Make their heart blaze and shine,

Bring them a love that will be mine.

My love will come here to stay,

Never ever to go away.

As my will, so mote it be."

Stay and meditate on the spell you just did, seeing it come true. After you have finished concentrating and visualizing, allow the candle to burn out. Soon your love will come to you.

Soul Mate Dream Vision

Unveil your destined love through a dream ritual that seeks to connect with your soul mate on a spiritual plane while you sleep.

Items Needed:

- 4 oz. Milk

- 1 tsp. Honey
- 3 Almonds
- 3 Raisins
- White Sachet

Directions:

Warm milk and add honey. Put the almonds and raisins into the sachet. Place sachet under your pillow. Drink your milk and honey before going to sleep. If there is a certain person you feel is your soul mate, think of that person while falling asleep. Your dream will tell you if they are "The One."

General Lover Attraction Spell

Attract a passionate partner without a specific person in mind using this spell that taps into universal love energies, inviting new romance.

Items Needed:

- 1 tsp. Catnip
- 1 tsp. Coriander
- 1 tsp. Ginger
- 1 tsp. Rosemary
- 1 tsp. Yarrow

Directions:

Mix herbs together. At sunset on a Friday when the moon is waxing (new moon to full moon), cast into a blazing fire. As the herbs burn, recite the following:

"My true love's face I've yet to see.

I know not what his (or her) name may be.

But soon his (her) heart well beat for me.

Come to me, my love.

As my will, so may it be.

Enchantress Candle Ritual

Ignite this spell to harness the powerful energies of candle magic, channeling your desires through focused flame for enchanting love and romantic attraction.

Items Needed:

- Red or Pink Witch-Shaped Candle
- A Sheet of Red or Pink Foil
- Patchouli Oil

Directions:

On Friday evening, candle on a sheet of foil (matching the candle's color). Etch the name of the man or woman you desire to love on the bottom of the candle. Anoint the candle with patchouli oil. Light the candle and say three times:

"Witch candle witch candle,

So bright with fire.

Summon the spirits,

Bring my desire."

Allow the candle to burn down about one inch a night (most witch candles are about 7.5" and needs to burn seven days). After it has burned all the way to the bottom, wrap the remains tightly with foil. Place under your bed for seven days and nights. After that time, throw wrapped bundle into moving body of water and say:

"Witch candle witch candle,

Your magic will bind.

Witch candle witch candle,

Let (name of the objective) be mine.

As my will, so mote it be."

Love Manifestation Box

Craft a love spell box to encapsulate your intentions and call forth romance by sealing in symbols, herbs, and affirmations that manifest passionate connections.

Items Needed:

- A Box
- Red candle
- Black candle
- Glue

Directions:

On a New Moon begin a hunt to find "love" objects to place inside the box, collecting nine objects in total. Charge them with your personal love energy. Place the objects and your box on your altar. Light the red and black candles. Pick up each object in your dominant hand and visualize the strongest emotions you have ever felt while in love. Glue each item into the box so that it stays in place. Let your intuition guide you to where to place each object. If you have a specific person in mind place his/her picture in the box as well. Keep the box in a magickal spot in your home. Every once in a while open the box to re-fuel the objects while letting some of the energy inside flow out into you.

Lover Attraction Spell

Draw a new romantic partner into your life with this potent spell, aligning your energy and desires to attract a lover who matches your intentions and passion.

Items Needed:

- Pink Candle
- Rose Quartz

Directions:

Inscribe the candle with the Ing ($\Diamond$), Gyfu ($\times$) and Beorc ($\triangleright$) Runes. Light the candle and place the stone beside the candle. Repeat three times:

"Three ladies came across the land,

Bringing love into my hand.

The first called him/her.

The second brought him/her.

Then third bound us together."

Allow candle to burn down completely. Place the stone among personal belongings of the objective.

Heart's Desire Manifestation

Use this spell to focus your intentions and manifest your heart's desire, aligning energies that help you gain the love and connection you seek.

Items Needed:

- 2 Red Candles
- 1 Gold Candle
- Olive Oil

- A Piece of White Cloth

Directions:

On a Full Moon night, Dress the candles with the oil, Place the gold candle before you. Take one red candle and place to the right and the other red candle directly in front of the gold candle. Think of him/her while you light the red and gold candles. Visualize and feel the love and power. Say:

"Here is (name of the objective)

This candle is him/her

As this flame burns

So does his spirit

I am his beloved

And he is mine."

Take the remains when the candles are burned completely and wrap them in the cloth. Keep it in a safe place.

Herbal Smoke Enchantment

Channel the power of sacred herbs with this smoke spell, cleansing your aura and attracting love energies through aromatic incense and purposeful affirmations.

Items Needed:

- Incense Burner
- Charcoal
- Dried Yarrow

Directions:

Sprinkle a pinch of yarrow onto lit charcoal. When the incense smoke begins to rise, visualize your lover's face in the smoke or glowing coal. Whisper these words over and over until you feel the magick happening.

"Magick herbs, burn in fire,

Bring to me my heart's desire."

Simple Love Knot Ritual

Harness the symbolic power of knots with this beginner-friendly spell, binding love intentions to weave passion and commitment into your relationships.

Items Needed:

- Pink Ribbon
- Red Ribbon
- Green Ribbon

Directions:

Grasp the ribbons and braid them together. Tie a knot firmly close to one end of the braid, visualizing your need for love. Tie a knot, after another up until you have secured seven knots. Carry or wear the cord on you until you discover your love. After you have found him or her, keep the cord in a secure place or bury it, throw in a lake, river or ocean.

Romantic Partner Enchantment

Cast this spell to strengthen your bond with a lover, infusing your relationship with passion, devotion, and romantic alignment for deeper intimacy.

Items Needed:

- Red Candle
- Lovers' Oil
- Lovers' Incense

Directions:

Dress the candle with the Lovers' oil, while you burn the incense. Say the following chant three times each night for five nights:

"I am overcome by burning love for this man/woman,

This love comes to me from Anteros,

Let this man/woman yearn only for me. Desire me; let his desire burn only for me.

Let this love come forward from the spirit and enter him/her.

Let him/her desire me, as he/she never has been desired before.

I love him/her, want him/her; he/she must feel the same desire for me.

Spirit of the air let him/her burn with love for me."

Lover Magnetism Ritual

Attract a compatible lover using this spell that aligns your energy with your intentions, inviting new romance into your life with an open heart.

Items Needed:

- Laurel Leaves
- A Dying Fire

Directions:

While sitting before a dying fire and gaze into it, clearing your mind of all but thoughts of your lover to have a small basket of laurel leaves between your knees. Keeping your gaze fixed on the fire, dip your left hand into the basket take out a handful of leaves, and toss them onto the fire. As they burst into flames, chant out loud:

"Laurel leaves that burn in the fire,

Draw to me my heart's desire.

Be it near or be it far,

As my will, so mote it be."

Wait for the flames to die down, and repeat. Do this three times.

Romantic Guidance Ritual

Seek clarity and insight into your love life with this spell, channeling divine guidance to illuminate your path toward harmonious relationships.

Items Needed:

- Full Moon
- Blood
- Clear Skies

Directions:

At night when the moon is full and the sky clear, prick your finger and distribute a few drops of blood around, saying:

"Sacred Moon

Watch over me from above.

Accept this offering,

May your light guide me to,

My one true love."

Basic Love Attraction Ritual

Cast this simple love spell to align your energy and intentions, creating a powerful magnetic aura that naturally draws new romance or strengthens existing relationships.

Items Needed:

- Picture of You
- Picture of Your Objective
- Open Fire
- Red String

Directions:

Write the name and day of birth of each individual on the back of their picture. Take the red string and bind the two pictures together, making sure their faces are staring at each other. When completed, put it into the fire, and as it burns say:

"Clotho, Lachesis, Atropos.

Sisters three, if it is your spiritual will,

Let these two be, happy together eternally.

As my will, so mote it be."

Passion Doorway Invitation

Invite passion into your life with this spell that opens your door to romantic energy, reigniting chemistry and sparking deep desire in new or current relationships.

Items Needed:

- 3 Drops Hot Pepper Sauce

- Dried Rosemary
- Black Peppercorns
- Dried Orris Root Pieces
- 3 drops Lavender Oil
- 3 cups of Rainwater (Gathered on Full Moon)

Directions:

Use two to three pinches of each herb and mix remaining ingredients together in a bowl while visualizing on drawing passion and love into your life. With your fingers, sprinkle the mixture around your front doorstep and walkway.

Triple Knot Devotion Charm

Harness the potent symbolism of the triple knot in this love spell, binding your intentions to cultivate unwavering devotion, passion, and unity in your romantic relationship.

Items Needed:

- 24 inches Red Ribbon
- Patchouli Oil
- Ylang-Ylang Oil

Directions:

Put a couple drops of each oil into your palms, rubbing them together. Rub the ribbon between your palms distributing the oils to anoint it. Space out three knots saying the line associated with that particular knot.

"With knot of one, my true love will come (first knot).

With the knot of two, the love shall be true (second knot).

With knot of three, so mote it be (third knot)."

Loop the knotted ribbon around a bedpost, bedside lamp or the doorknob to your bedroom. Don't knot it though; you don't need any extra knots in there.

Romantic Talisman Pouch

Create a love pouch filled with magical herbs and charms, carrying it with you to enhance your romantic aura and attract passionate connections wherever you go.

Items Needed:

- Catnip
- Jasmine Flowers
- Small Pink Pouch
- 4 Pink Candles
- Cauldron
- Paper
- Pen

Directions:

On your altar, place the 4 candles at the north, east, south, and west with the cauldron in the middle. Put the jasmine and catnip in the cauldron. On the paper, print out the points you wish in a relationship as well as a partner. Sign your name to it, and fold it.

Position the paper in the cauldron, and light it, burning mostly the paper. While the paper burns, say:

"With the power of fire and my words,

Bring me the love, the love I deserve."

Repeat until the paper is fully burned Stir the ashes in with the herbs, and pour them into the pink bag. Tie the bag closed, and carry it with you.

Enchanting Love Spell Jar

Craft this love spell bottle to amplify your romantic energy, sealing powerful intentions in an enchanted jar to manifest passion and attract soulful connections.

Items Needed:

- Rosewater
- Handful Dried Rose Petals
- Pinch Dried Lavender
- Pinch Sandalwood
- 2 Oz. Bottle with Cap or Cork

Directions:

Hold the rose petals in your hands and empower them with love. Place herbs in the bottle. Slowly fill the bottle with rose water. Seal bottle with cap or cork. Hold bottle to your heart saying these words:

"Flowers drenched with love

Drench me with love."

Keep the love spell bottle in your bedroom.

Attraction Visibility Ritual

Perform this spell to radiate an aura of attraction, boosting your self-confidence and magnetic charm so you are seen more attractively by potential partners.

Items Needed:

- Fresh Rose Petals
- 6 Pink Candles
- Lavender Incense

Directions:

Fill your bathtub with water. Sprinkle the fresh rose petals into the water. Light the pink candles and place around your bathtub. Light your lavender incense. As you lie in the water, meditate and visualize the image that you would like to project. Say:

"Earth, Fire, Spirit, Air, Sea,

Let the Goddess' beauty shine through me."

Take it easy and relax as you concentrate on yourself.

Full Moon Wiccan Romance Ritual

Harness the powerful energy of the full moon with this Wiccan love spell, amplifying your romantic intentions to manifest new passion or strengthen an existing relationship.

Items Needed:

- Red Candle
- Pink Candle
- Dried Basil
- Ground Cinnamon
- Two Apple Seeds
- A Moonstone Crystal
- A Rose Quartz Crystal
- A Red Fabric or Cloth
- Pink Cord

Directions:

Gather ingredients in a sacred space beneath a full moon, casting your circle. Light both candles, and laying the red material in front of you. Pass the moonstone over the fires of both candles, and then lay on the cloth. Repeat with the rose quartz. Get the two apple seeds, and declare:

"In the bright of this full moon,

I plant the seeds of our love."

Visualize a pink energy emitting from the crystals as you place the seeds on the fabric as it feeds the seeds with energy of love. Scatter the seeds and stones with the cinnamon and basil. Pull the corners of the red fabric together, keeping the herbs, stones, and seeds inside. Wrap the pink cord three times around the bag, before tying it with three knots. Afterward, say:

"As my will, so mote it be."

Keep your charm bag near to you at all times with the purpose of attracting love into your life.

Tea Light Attraction Charm

Illuminate your romantic path with this tea light love spell, channeling focused intentions through soft candlelight to draw affection and meaningful connections.

Items Needed:

- 1 White Tea Light Candle

Directions:

Light candle and place it on the window sill at night.

This will represent you calling out to your love.

Pink Candle Romance Enchantment

Ignite a pink candle to radiate love and warmth, setting the stage for deepening intimacy and inviting harmonious relationships into your life.

Items Needed:

- Pink Candle
- Virgin Olive Oil

Directions:

Place the pink candle it on a table or your altar. Dress with olive oil. While dressing the candle, charge it with love and desire. After dressing the candle, take a knife and carve what it is you want into the candle. Light candle and let burn out.

Self-Assurance Candle Ritual

Light this confidence candle to boost self-esteem and enhance your aura, helping you radiate self-assurance and attract positive connections effortlessly.

Items Needed:

- Pink Candle
- Pink and White Rose Petals
- Spring Water

Directions:

Improving your own opinion of yourself can go a long way in giving you confidence in any part of your life. On an altar or table, make a ring of flower petals and set up the candle in the center. Before you light it, think of your best traits and concentrate on those for a few minutes. Light the candle. Repeat the following:

"May my own light shine,

With perfect love and sweet divine."

Take a long drink of water, to cleanse out your negative thoughts of yourself. Leave the candle to burn out on its own

Friendship Bonding Flame

Cast this friendship candle spell to strengthen your bonds with friends, nurturing loyalty and trust while inviting new supportive relationships into your circle.

Items Needed:

- Pink Candle
- Good Luck/Friendship Oil
- Pink Silk Ribbon
- White Silk Ribbon

Directions:

Anoint the pink candle with Good Luck oil while thinking of the friends you want to make. Visualize yourself laughing with them, going out with them. Really see yourself with them.

Light your candle while you continue your visualization, seeing things that are important to you in a friend: trust, honesty, humor, etc.

When this is completed, take your two pieces of silk ribbon and wind them together. While doing this, think of bringing that friend closer to you. You are binding that friend to you, making them loyal to you, the way any good friend should be. Do not bind a specific person to you, since it harms the other person's free will. Only bind the idea of the perfect friend to you.

Once you have done this, tie the ribbon to the base of your candle. The candle's light will be a guiding light to bring friendship to you and another person. Meditate on the spell, sending your energies out to bring that perfect friend to you. Let your candle burn all the way down.

Luminous Bulb Enchantment

Plant powerful intentions with this bulb spell, symbolizing growth and renewal as you cultivate energy to manifest love, prosperity, or any desire you wish to see bloom.

Items Needed:

- New Flower Pot
- Soil
- Any Type of Plant Bulb

Directions:

Plant the bulb in the pot making sure you use plenty of soil. Recite over plant each day:

"As this root grows,

And as your blossom grows,

May his/her heart be turned to me.

As my will, so mote it be."

Dreamscape Romance Vision

Cast this love dream spell to align your subconscious with your heart's desires, inviting romantic visions through dreams that guide you toward your ideal partner.

Items Needed:

- ½ tsp. Vinegar
- White Wine
- Distilled Gin

Directions:

Before going to bed place in your chalice mixture of spring water, drops of white wine, and gin which is stirred with the finger of the dominant hand while focusing. Drink potion before going to bed.

Knot Binding Ritual

Tie this love knot spell to weave a magical bond of passion and unity, binding your intentions to manifest a secure and loving relationship.

Items Needed:

- A Pink Piece of Yarn
- A Red Piece of Yarn
- A White Piece of Yarn

Directions:

Tie a knot near one end of the braid as you visualize a new love arriving in your life. As you tie the knot, say the following prayer or another prayer or chant that is meaningful to you:

"Venus, Queen of Love, divine;

Bring me the love to me that's destined to be mine."

Braid the three strings together as you continue to visualize the perfect romantic partner falling deeply in love with you as you fall in love with him/her. Really try to feel the emotions of the two of you being happy together.

Visualize being romantic, kissing and smiling. Tie another knot and repeat the prayer as you continue the visualization. Do this a total of seven times (knot & prayer, braid & visualize, knot & prayer), until you have seven knots in the cord. Keep the knotted string with you until you find your perfect love. After you have found love, keep the cord in a safe place. If someday you decide you want to end the relationship, simple burn and release yourself and your objective.

Magnetic Love Attraction

Channel your desires to attract love with this spell, aligning your energy to draw a partner whose heart resonates with your own romantic intentions.

Items Needed:

- Candle of Your Favorite Color
- Red Candle
- Music

Directions:

Play some romantic music that means something to you. Be sure that the music does not contain songs that you may associate with someone Light the candle of your favorite candle to represent you. Light the red candle to represent your objective. Place candles on your altar seven inches apart. Burn candles ten minutes a day visualizing your objective. Move candles an inch towards each other. By the seventh day, they should be touching. This will draw a new love to you.

Blood Bond Enchantment

Create a sacred connection with this blood spell, ethically sealing your intentions to build an unbreakable bond with a partner through mutual devotion and commitment.

Items Needed:

- Cone of Patchouli Incense
- Red Apple
- Your Blood
- Objective Blood
- Athame
- Silver Pin

Directions:

To do this spell, you must have the full cooperation of your lover. You must do it together. Drip a drop or two of your blood on a cone of patchouli incense saying:

"Blood of (your name),

Love of (your name)."

Have your lover, do the same, dripping a drop or two of his/her blood on the incense saying:

"Blood of (his/her name),

Love of (his/her name)."

After lighting the incense, pass the red apple through the smoke three times. Lay the apple on its side and cut in half with Athame exposing the seeds in the center. Eat one half and give the other to your lover.

3

TO MAINTAIN LOVE

Maintaining love in a relationship is as essential as the initial spark that ignites the romance. It is a continuous process that requires effort, commitment, and an understanding of the dynamic nature of human relationships. Various lenses emphasize this significance, including psychological well-being, societal stability, and personal growth.

Psychological Well-Being

From a psychological standpoint, the maintenance of love is crucial for emotional stability and happiness. Studies have shown that individuals in long-term, loving relationships report higher levels of personal satisfaction and mental health. Love provides a support system that helps individuals weather the storms of life, offering emotional security and reducing feelings of anxiety and depression. The act of maintaining love —through communication, empathy, and mutual respect— fosters an environment where individuals can express their feelings without fear of judgment, enhancing emotional intimacy and trust.

Societal Stability

On a broader scale, maintaining love within relationships contributes to societal stability. Families founded on enduring relationships provide a more stable upbringing for children, who benefit from the emotional and economic support of a cohesive family unit. These children are more likely to develop into well-adjusted adults, contributing positively to society. Stable relationships reduce social issues like loneliness and isolation, which are increasingly recognized as significant health risks in modern societies.

Personal Growth

Maintaining love also promotes personal growth. Relationships are not static; they grow as people grow and change. Staying in love means adapting to these changes within oneself and one's partner. This adaptation requires self-awareness, patience, and, often, a willingness to compromise. Through these processes, individuals learn about themselves, develop resilience, and gain a deeper understanding of what it means to share life with another person. Each challenge faced and overcome together can strengthen the bond, deepening the love and commitment.

Efforts in Maintenance

Effort is the cornerstone of maintaining love. It encompasses various actions and attitudes, including:

- **Communication:** Open, honest dialogue is fundamental. It involves not only talking but also listening. Effective communication helps prevent misunderstandings and resolves conflicts before they escalate.

- **Appreciation:** Regularly expressing gratitude and appreciation for one's partner fosters a positive relationship atmosphere. Simple acknowledgments of a partner's efforts and qualities can significantly boost relationship satisfaction.
- **Quality Time:** Spending quality time together, whether on shared interests or simple daily routines, strengthens emotional connections and keeps the relationship vibrant and engaging.
- **Physical Intimacy:** Maintaining physical closeness through affectionate touch or sexual intimacy reinforces the physical bond between partners and promotes hormonal responses that increase feelings of love and contentment.
- **Resolving Conflicts:** It is essential to learn to manage and resolve conflicts constructively, without resentment or anger. Every relationship encounters challenges, and handling these positively can prevent harm.

Cultural and Personal Variations

The importance of maintaining love and the methods employed can vary significantly across different cultures and personal beliefs. In some cultures, love is more deeply intertwined with familial and societal obligations. In contrast, in others, personal satisfaction and emotional fulfillment are prioritized. Understanding these differences is crucial in a globalized world where cross-cultural relationships are common.

The maintenance of love is vital not only for the well-being of individuals, but also for the health of societies. It requires continuous effort and adaptation, reflecting the dynamic nature of human relationships. By committing to the ongoing nurturing of love, individuals can ensure that their relationships endure and flourish, bringing lifelong satisfaction and joy.

Long-Term Love Spells

Spells to maintain love are essential for nurturing the bonds of an existing relationship, helping couples preserve the harmony and joy they have cultivated. These spells focus on strengthening trust, enhancing communication, and fostering deeper intimacy to ensure that the initial spark of love develops into a lasting, vibrant connection. They encompass rituals and practices that address common challenges, such as waning passion, misunderstandings, external stresses like work or family, and even personal insecurities, offering couples the magical tools to fortify their relationship.

Approaching spells to maintain love with genuine intentions and an open heart is crucial. It's not just about preventing problems, but proactively celebrating the relationship's strengths. As you explore these spells, remember that their magic lies in the continuous efforts made by both partners to grow together with patience, kindness, and understanding. To approach these spells with genuine intentions, it's important to reflect on your feelings and desires, and to ensure that your actions align with your true intentions for the relationship.

Unconditional Love Sustainer": Cast this spell to maintain unconditional love in your relationship, fostering understanding, trust, and deep emotional bonds that withstand life's challenges.

Items Needed:

- White Candle
- Pink Candle
- Black Candle
- Any Choice Incense

Directions:

Looking up at the Full Moon, light the candles and incense. Say:

"Destinies have blessed my home,

Destinies have blessed my heart.

Destinies have blessed my loved ones;

I give my thanks with a simple heart.

I thank the Goddess for my life; I thank the Goddess for my love.

I thank the Goddess for continued blessings already on their way.

As my will, so mote it be."

Rekindle Lost Romance Ritual": Use this spell to bring back a lover, reigniting the flame of passion and healing past wounds to restore a harmonious and loving partnership.

Items Needed:

- Two White Candles
- Photo of Lover
- Photo of Yourself Smiling
- Chamomile Tea Bag
- A Piece of Blue Material

Directions:

At 8:00 in the evening light the candles and taking a few deep breaths to relax. Imagine a peaceful scene. Hold the picture of the person in your hand and repeat these words:

"With the light of this flame,

I will light your desire.

I will speak your name,

You will feel my fire.

Love I feel,

You will see.

As my will, so mote it be."

Say his/her name three times placing your picture face down on top of his/hers so that the two images are together. Wrap the two pictures along with the tea bag in the blue cloth. Put the package in a safe place. Light the candles at 8 p.m. each night and say his/her name three times. The spell should work in three weeks.

Lover Return Enchantment": Invoke this spell to draw back a former partner, mending broken ties and rekindling the affectionate connection that once united your hearts.

Items Needed:

- Basil Leaves
- Silver Pin
- A Circular Piece of White Silk

Directions:

Burn some basil leaves collecting the ashes. Prick your finger with a sterile silver pin. Write your name and your objective's on a piece of white silk. Draw a circle around the names with the ashes of basil. As you fold crumble the silk command your lover to come to you. Stick the pin in the silk to hold it together and bury it in a sacred place at midnight on the third night of the waxing moon.

Harmony Restoring Spell": Cast this spell to stop an argument and restore peace by dispelling negative energy, fostering understanding, and encouraging open communication in your relationship.

Items Needed:

- Glass Purple Plate
- Picture of Objective

Directions:

Place picture face down on the plate for about fifteen minutes.

The person will either call or come by with offers of an apology in about 24 hours. If not, do spell again for about fifteen minutes. If by the third time you still haven't heard from them, give them a call or go see them. Their feelings will have changed.

White Magick Problem Solver": Perform this white magick spell to remove obstacles and negativity, invoking powerful protective energy to clear problems and bring clarity to challenging situations.

Items Needed:

White Candle

Pink Candle

Matches

Parchment Paper

Pencil

Directions:

Etch on the white candle your name; the pink candle will be your partner's name. Ignite the white candle, then the pink candle. For the thirty minutes focus on the candles as it burns. Visualizing your circumstances and how much you want for those problems to resolve themselves and the harmony and love you want to draw into your relationship.

Take the pencil and sketch three hearts on the parchment paper. Get the white candle and let the wax drop on the hearts as you are imagining and concentrating on what you will transform and how the great deal of love you are ready to give your partner. After you have coated the hearts with wax snuff or blow the white candle. Hold the pink candle and drip wax on the hearts at the same time as you are visualizing and concentrating on what you desire to have in response of your partner.

After you have coated the hearts with wax snuff the pink candle. Do again for seven days with the same piece of paper except draw new hearts each day. Let the candles burn themselves out after the seventh day. Keep the parchment paper in a hidden place where no one can ever discover it.

Conflict Resolution Enchantment": Use this spell to clear an argument, calming heightened emotions and inviting constructive dialogue to bring balance and harmony back into your relationship.

Items Needed:

- Bay Leaf
- Small Envelope

- Yellow Candle
- A Fire Safe Container or Bowl

Directions:

Write your name on one side of the envelope, and your aim's name on the other. Place the bay leaf inside and seal it. Light the candle and hold the envelope in the flame until it burns. Place into fire-safe container or bowl.

Distant Lover Connection Ritual": Cast this spell to send a loving message to your distant partner, strengthening your bond and ensuring your intentions reach their heart across any distance.

- **Items Needed:**
- White Crystal Quartz
- Picture of Your Lover

Directions:

Take a photo of your lover and set the quartz over the photo. Concentrate and visualize your message into the quartz crystal and picture. Feel your energy and the message being sent to your lover.

Secure Love Enchantment": Invoke this spell to make love secure, reinforcing your relationship with intentions of loyalty, trust, and unwavering emotional stability.

Items Needed:

- Apple (with center cored)
- Cinnamon
- Rose Petals
- Hair from Your Lover or Spouse

- Your Hair
- Pink Ribbon
- White Ribbon
- Three Pink Candles
- White Cloth

Directions:

Take a lock of hair from your spouse or lover tying a pink ribbon around it. A lock of your own hair secured with a white ribbon. Light the three pink candles and then set the hair in an emptied apple along with a dash of ground cinnamon, 7 rose petals. Pass the apple through the light of each candle while visualizing yourself and your spouse/lover. Wrap the apple in a piece of white material. Bury it under the window where you slumber. Helps strengthen the existing bond between the two of you.

Peaceful Waters Ritual": Perform this spell to smooth the waters, calming conflicts and restoring peace and understanding between you and your partner for harmonious love.

Items Needed:

- A Large Bowl
- Salt
- Rosemary
- A Key
- 12" Piece of String

Directions:

Tie the key to the string. Fill the bowl with water adding a pinch or two of both salt and rosemary. Give it a mix with your finger to bring the water rippling. Repeat:

"Smooth the waters with my friend,

I need our troubles to end."

Watching the water, dangle the key over the surface and recite the words until the water is still. Wear the key around your neck for three days and making sure you are putting the resolution into defining what may be amiss with your friendship.

Reunion Flame Candle Spell": Light this return-to-me candle spell to rekindle the flame with a former lover, encouraging reconciliation and guiding their path back to your embrace.

Items Needed:

- Pink, Red or White Candle
- Vanilla Oil
- Red String

Directions:

Inscribe your initials on the candle and then your loved one's initials on yours. Not above your initials, but on them. Anoint the candle with vanilla oil.

Tie a bow on the candle with the string so that the bow lies over the initials. Light the candle and allow it to burn until it reaches where the initials are. Snuff out the candle and set it on your altar finishing it when your loved one returns. Each day, add a little oil to the initials each day until then.

Daily Practices and Spells

Incorporating daily practices and spells into one's routine is a powerful tool for maintaining and enhancing one's magical path. These daily practices go beyond simply performing spells; By engaging in daily practices, practitioners can ground themselves, refine their focus, and strengthen their connection to the mystical energies that they work with. Utilizing this disciplined approach can greatly amplify the effectiveness of complex spells and rituals, as well as establish a steady framework for personal growth and spiritual discovery.

The Role of Daily Practices in Magic

Engaging in daily practices serves multiple purposes: maintaining a magical mindset, cleansing and protecting personal energy, and keeping skills sharp and focused. Just as athletes train regularly to keep their bodies in peak condition, magicians practice daily to keep their spiritual and magical faculties finely tuned. These routines can vary widely depending on one's traditions, beliefs, and goals. Incorporate practices that align with your beliefs and goals on your spiritual path. However, they typically include elements of meditation, energy cleansing, protective warding, and gratitude.

Meditation and Centering

Meditation is a cornerstone of many magical practices. It helps clear the mind, focus on intent, and connect with higher spiritual energies. Daily meditation can involve simple breath work, guided visualizations, or mantra recitations. Consistency and being present are crucial. Centering, a practice often paired with meditation, involves aligning one's spiritual, mental, and physical states to achieve balance and inner harmony, which is essential for effective spellcasting.

Energy Cleansing and Protection

Engaging in energy cleansing daily is essential for experiencing a sense of security and protection. You can achieve this through various methods such as smudging with sage, Palo Santo, or other herbs, using sounds like bells or singing bowls, or visualizing a light washing over and purifying your body. To protect against negative energies or unwanted spiritual entities, it is important to establish protective barriers or wards after cleansing. This can involve visualizing a protective sphere around the home or carrying protective amulets or talismans, providing a reassuring sense of safety in the magical journey.

Casting Daily Spells

Daily spells can be simple yet powerful. Common daily spells include:

- **Affirmation Spells:** Using positive affirmations charged with intent for personal empowerment, such as affirmations for confidence, peace, or success.
- **Candle Magic:** Lighting specific candles while focusing on intent or desire, using color symbolism to enhance the spell (e.g., green for growth, blue for healing).
- **Herbal Magic:** Creating small sachets of herbs for specific purposes like love, protection, or prosperity and carrying them throughout the day.
- **Gratitude Rituals:** Maintaining a gratitude ritual can manifest more positivity. This might involve writing things you are grateful for and burning the paper to release the intentions to the universe.

The Benefits of Consistency

The consistent application of daily practices and spells fosters a deep and resonant connection to the magical forces at work in the practitioner's life. Developing a rhythm through consistency helps practitioners become attuned to the subtle ebb and flow of magical energies. Over time, this can lead to a more intuitive practice where the practitioner can respond fluidly to spiritual and magical needs without extensive ritual preparation.

Daily practices and spells are not just routines; they are the transformative building blocks of disciplined magickal practice. They prepare the practitioner for more complex workings, protect against negative influences, and enhance personal and spiritual growth. By adhering to these daily routines, individuals can sustain a strong bond with the mystical realm, guaranteeing a powerful and meaningful magical expedition. This daily commitment to the craft is not merely a practice but a way of living magically every day, inspiring and motivating practitioners to embrace the transformative power of magic.

4

THE ENDING OF LOVE

When love ends, it can be a profound and often painful transition for those involved. The dissolution of a relationship, whether by mutual agreement or unilateral decision, marks a significant change in one's life trajectory and emotional landscape. While challenging, this phase is also a crucial period for personal growth, healing, and eventual renewal.

Emotional Impact of Love Ending

The immediate aftermath of a relationship's end is typically characterized by a tumult of emotions. Feelings of sadness, betrayal, loneliness, and anger are common. These emotions are part of the grieving process, as individuals mourn not just the loss of a partner, but also the shared dreams and plans for the future that will no longer come to fruition. Psychological studies like the end of a romantic relationship to experiencing a bereavement. Like any significant loss, it requires a period of change and healing.

Understanding and Acceptance

Understanding why love ended is a crucial step in the healing process. Sometimes, the reasons are apparent, such as incompatible life goals or values. Other times, they might be less apparent, involving a gradual drift apart or unresolved recurrent conflicts. Whatever the cause, coming to terms with these reasons is essential for. Acceptance does not imply immediate relief from pain, but acknowledging the reality of the situation without being imprisoned by it.

The Role of Reflection

When love ends, reflection plays a pivotal role. It involves examining the relationship to understand what worked and what did not. This reflection is not about assigning blame but about learning from the experience. Understanding one's contributions to both the successes and failures of the relationship can be enlightening and instrumental in personal growth. It helps individuals identify patterns that may need to be addressed, improving their future relational dynamics.

Growth and Self-Discovery

The end of a relationship often prompts a period of self-discovery. Freed from the compromises of a partnership, individuals can explore their desires, interests, and aspirations that might have been sidelined. This can be a time for personal development, where one can take up new hobbies, travel, or pursue educational or career ambitions that were previously on hold. This growth is vital not only for recovering from the loss but also for building a more prosperous, more fulfilled life.

Moving Forward

Moving forward after a relationship ends involves both healing from the past and gradually opening oneself to the possibilities of the future. It is important to give oneself time to heal and not rush into new relationships prematurely. Rebuilding one's life after a breakup means cultivating a solid support network of friends and family, engaging in activities that boost one's spirits and confidence, and possibly seeking professional help if coping becomes too difficult.

Forgiveness and Release

Forgiveness, both of oneself and the former partner, can significantly aid the healing process. It involves letting go of grudges and bitterness, which can be detrimental to one's mental health. Releasing these negative emotions makes room for more positive experiences and relationships in the future.

Renewed Sense of Self

Ultimately, the end of love can lead to a renewed sense of self. It can teach resilience, highlight personal strength, and clarify what one truly values in a relationship. While the journey may be fraught with challenges, it also holds the promise of newfound wisdom and a deeper appreciation for love when it comes around again.

When love ends, it signifies not just an end but also a beginning—a chance to rediscover and reinvent oneself, to learn from experiences, and to approach future relationships with a deeper understanding and respect. The pain of a breakup is undeniable, but so is the potential for emerging from it more whole, focused, and ready to love again.

Release Spells

Release spells serve a vital role in the realm of magical practices, especially for closing chapters and letting go of connections that no longer serve us. Let's remember that the specific rituals and practices mentioned here originate from certain cultural and spiritual traditions. While the principles of release and healing are universal, the specific methods may vary. These spells serve the purpose of promoting emotional, spiritual, and sometimes physical release, allowing individuals to sever ties with past relationships, negative patterns, or burdensome emotions. The process of casting release spells is thoroughly cathartic, offering a ritualistic means to cleanse one's life of unwanted attachments and energies.

Here, we look into a variety of release spells, each specifically designed to help practitioners relinquish different bonds. From simple cord-cutting rituals to more elaborate ceremonies aimed at clearing away residual energies left by past lovers, the spells we discuss here are potent tools for those seeking closure and renewal. The key to these spells is the intention to release, which must be clear and strong, driven by a deep-seated desire to heal and move forward, and to embrace the transformative potential of these practices.

Approaching these spells, it is crucial to do so with a mindset of compassion and forgiveness—towards oneself and others. Release spells are not solely about letting go but also about paving the way for new beginnings and positive changes, making them a significant stride in one's personal and spiritual growth.

Ending of Love Spells

The ending of love spells, sometimes known as separation or release spells, is a crucial yet delicate aspect of magical practice. Specifically, practitioners design it to facilitate the respectful and intentional conclusion of relationships that no longer serve both partners. These spells aim to help individuals move forward with grace and find peace after a breakup, rather than being cast to invoke harm or create unnecessary turmoil. It's important to note that the ethical considerations of using these spells include respecting the other person's feelings and consent, and ensuring that the decision to end the relationship is mutual and well-considered.

Approach these spells with clarity and compassion, ensuring that the intention is to end the relationship respectfully while fostering personal healing. Remember that the purpose of these spells is to gently untangle the threads of the past and enable both partners to move forward toward brighter, healthier futures, not to manipulate or control the other person.

Release & Renew Ritual": Cast this spell to let a lover go, freeing yourself from past emotional ties with compassion, opening the way for personal healing and new romantic opportunities.

Items Needed:

- Picture of You and Your Ex
- Your Athame

Directions:

Cast your circle as usual during a waning moon. Place the picture of you and your ex on your altar. With no thoughts of retaliation or retribution, take your Athame and remove your ex out of the picture. Place the picture of him/her into the fire and think of a happy and positive life without this person. Bury the ashes in a suitable spot.

Ex Separation Freeze Spell": Perform this freezing spell to keep your ex at bay, establishing healthy boundaries that protect your emotional well-being while allowing you to move forward.

Items Needed:

A Piece of Paper

Small Plastic Bag

Water

Freezer

Ex's Full Name

Directions:

At Midnight on a Full Moon, Write the full name of your ex on a piece of paper. Crumple the paper into a ball and put it into the plastic bag along with the water. Carefully hold the container up to the moon and say:

"Light of the Moon,

Hear me well shout.

Make him/her gone,

Freeze him/her out.

The spell is cast,

The magick will last.

As my will so mote it be."

Put the container into the freezer compartment of your fridge, in a place where you know it won't be disturbed or found. Leave it in your fridge for as long as it takes. Then - and only then - throw it all away far, far away from your house.

Negative Partner Banishing Chant": Use this chant to banish bad lovers and their energy from your life, clearing your space of harmful influences and creating room for healthier relationships.

Directions:

During the Waning Moon Phase, visualize and chant:

"**Lovers who don't know how to love,**

Go away, I'll find new love.

Lovers who don't treat me right,

Go away move out of sight."

Lunar Release Ritual": Use this moon magick break-up spell to harness lunar energy, releasing a toxic relationship while empowering yourself with the moon's transformative power to find peace and new beginnings.

Items Needed:

- 1 Black Candle
- 3 Black Cat Hairs
- Parchment Paper
- Small Bowl with 13 tbsp. of Water
- 3 tbsp. Epsom Salt
- A Fire Safe Container or Bowl

Directions:

In the Waning Moon period, cleanse and consecrate your candle. Write the couple's names who you wish to break up on the parchment paper. Mix the water with the Epsom Salt until it is dissolved.

Ignite the black candle. Hold the black candle up with your dominant hand as you begin to visualize the couple fighting. With the parchment paper at the front of you, focus on your intention allowing 13 drops of wax fall on the parchment paper. Place the cat hairs on parchment paper, pressed into the wax. Dip your fingers into the Epsom salt mixture. With the moisture of this mixture, sprinkle the drops of it onto the parchment paper. Repeat this seven times.

Snuff candle out. Burn completely the parchment paper together with the cat hairs in fire safe bowl or container. On the following full moon Light the remaining candle until it has burned out. Allowing this will seal the spell, as well as increasing its power.

Wiccan Separation Enchantment": Invoke this Wicca break-up spell to respectfully end a relationship, freeing yourself and your partner with positive intentions and creating space for growth and renewal.

Items Needed:

- 1 tsp. Cayenne Pepper
- 1 tsp. Salt
- 6 Drops Garlic Oil
- Parchment Paper
- Pencil
- Black Candle
- Matches

Directions:

During the Waning Moon Phase, cleanse and consecrate your candle. Light the candle. Write the names of the couple you wish to break up on the parchment paper. Drop three drops of garlic oil on both of the names. Add cayenne pepper and salt. Hold the black candle up with your dominant hand as you begin to visualize the couple separating and breaking up.

Using the candle drop the wax on top of their names, dried herbs, and oil continue to visualize. After you have covered all with wax, snuff or blow out the candle and state:

"As I pass on my will,

This spell has now been received,

As I will, so mote it be."

Snuff candle. Wrap the parchment paper about the items. You can burn packet, bury it or throw in a lake, river or ocean. Light the left over candle on the subsequent full moon while waiting for it to burn itself out.

Healing Rituals

Healing rituals within the realm of love magic are crucial for addressing the emotional and spiritual wounds that often accompany relationships. From recovering from a past relationship to resolving conflicts and nurturing existing relationships, these rituals offer a contemplative and transformative way to heal and grow. This chapter examines different healing rituals, offering advice on tapping into their power to heal emotional wounds and enhance connections.

Understanding Healing in Love Magic

Healing is a fundamental aspect of any meaningful relationship. It requires more than just fixing what is broken; In love magic, healing rituals are not just practices but profound expressions of the desire to nurture and restore harmony.

Key Components of Healing Rituals in Love Magic

I. **Intention Setting:** Every healing ritual starts with a clear and pure intention. This intention could be to release old wounds, forgive past hurts, or strengthen the resilience of a relationship. For the ritual to have its full healing potential, intentions should be set with honesty and vulnerability.

2. **Purification:** Before undertaking any ritual, especially those involving emotional healing, it is important to purify the space and the individuals involved. You can achieve this by smudging sage, palo santo, or using sound vibrations like bells or singing bowls. Purification helps to clear out negative energy and create a safe, sacred space for healing to occur.

3. **Rituals for Self-Healing:** Often, the health of our relationships can reflect our own emotional state. Self-healing rituals are crucial and can include meditation, affirmations, or creating amulets for self-love and worth. Crystals such as rose quartz or rhodonite can enhance these rituals, as they are known for their properties of promoting love and compassion.

4. **Couple's Healing Rituals:** Couple's healing rituals can be beneficial for relationships undergoing strain or past trauma. Both partners may actively participate in healing rituals, such as creating a love sigil, performing a forgiveness ceremony, or joining a guided healing circle.

5. **Ritual Tools and Symbols:** Utilizing tools such as candles, herbs, and oils that correspond to love and healing can amplify the effects of the ritual. Pink candles for love, lavender for peace, and chamomile for harmony are just a few examples. Symbols of unity, such as intertwined circles or the infinity symbol, can also be powerful.

Sample Healing Ritual for Love

A simple yet effective healing ritual for love might involve the following steps:

1. **Create a Sacred Space:** Arrange a comfortable and clean area where you won't be disturbed. Light pink candles and use rose incense to invite love energies.

2. **Write Intentions and Forgiveness:** Both partners write down their intentions for healing on a piece of paper, along with any declarations of forgiveness. If comfortable, they can share these with each other.

3. **Meditation and Visualization:** Sit face-to-face, hold hands, and close your eyes. Visualize a healing light enveloping both of you, soothing old wounds and strengthening your bond.

4. **Seal the Ritual:** Exchange tokens of love (e.g., stones or written vows) and conclude with a heartfelt affirmation spoken together, such as "Together, we heal, we love, we grow."

Healing rituals in love magic are a gentle yet powerful way to address the complexities of relationships. By consistently practicing these methods, couples can guarantee that their relationship not only endures but flourishes when confronted with obstacles, fostering a stronger bond and a deeper comprehension of one another.

5

MAGICKAL RECIPES

Magickal love recipes offer practitioners a tangible way to infuse their relationships with the energies of love, passion, and harmony. Drawing from age-old traditions, these recipes include blends, brews, and concoctions designed to align your intentions with the natural energies found in herbs, oils, and other powerful ingredients. Whether seeking to ignite a new flame, rekindle passion, or fortify an existing bond, these recipes provide a meaningful and creative approach to love magic.

As you explore these recipes, remember that their potency lies in the energy and intention you bring to the process. By blending the ingredients with focus and a clear heart, you'll find these magickal recipes not only enhance your love life but also deepen your connection to the natural world and its mystical energies. Your active participation and intention are key to their success.

Each recipe will basically be one size which you can divide and store extra. Just like cooking, you can, of course, adjust the measurements. I go by scent myself. Just like cooking.

Creating Your Oils

If you have allergies or sensitive skin, it's crucial to always test essential oils (including base oils) before using them in blends or applying them topically. This simple step, every time you purchase a new oil, can provide a sense of security, ensuring it won't cause irritation or an allergic reaction.

When creating your blends, follow these guidelines to ensure optimal fragrance and safe usage:

Ingredient Proportions: The proportions provided are recommendations. The primary scent is the first ingredient. As you move down the list, subsequent oils are used in smaller quantities.

Blending Process: Add your essential oils to a base oil like coconut, jojoba, or grapeseed. Measure out 1/4 cup of base oil in a clean glass jar. It's important to use clean glass jars to ensure hygiene and prevent contamination. Add essential oils one drop at a time while gently stirring to achieve the desired fragrance intensity.

Storage Tips: Store your blends in a cool, dark, and dry place, away from direct heat, moisture, and light. This will help preserve their quality and potency. Essential oil blends typically have a shelf life of [6 months to 1 year], so it's important to use or discard them accordingly.

Labeling: Properly label your oil blends, including the date of creation and the ingredients used. This will help you track their freshness and keep them organized. You can also [mark the date of expiration or the recommended use-by date] to further ensure the quality of your blends.

By following these safety and storage tips, you can enjoy the benefits of essential oil blends while ensuring your oils remain fresh and effective.

Attraction Oil Blend

Create this come-to-me oil to attract romance into your life, blending fragrant herbs and essential oils that draw in passionate partners and encourage new connections.

Items Needed:

- 4 drops Patchouli Oil
- 2 drops Bergamot Oil
- 2 drops Damiana Oil

Romantic Lover's Oil

Craft this lover's oil for enhancing intimacy and devotion, using aromatic ingredients that foster closeness and deepen the affectionate bond with your partner.

Items Needed:

- 4 drops Ylang-Ylang Oil
- 2 drops Rose Oil

Desire Potion Elixir

Mix this desire oil to ignite passion, infusing it with seductive herbs and essential oils that amplify sensual energy and awaken mutual longing.

Items Needed:

- 3 drops Lavender Oil
- 2 drops Orange Oil
- 1 drop Rose Oil
- 1 drop Lemon Oil

Romantic Essence Oil

Craft this scent of romance blend to envelop yourself in an alluring fragrance, attracting affection and inspiring desire with its delicate, enchanting aroma.

Items Needed:

- 2 drop Orange Oil
- 2 drops Cedar Oil
- 3 drops Sage Oil
- 1 drops Vanilla Oil

Bond-Strengthening Elixir

Create this build-a-bond oil to nurture unity and loyalty, using herbs and essential oils that encourage deeper emotional intimacy and commitment.

Items Needed:

- 6 drops Rose Oil
- 7 drops Ylang-Ylang Oil
- 3 drops Ginger Oil
- 4 drops Rosemary Oil

This is a mixture you can use to help strengthen an existing love.

Love Magnetism Oil

Blend this drawing love oil to amplify your romantic aura, harnessing potent botanical ingredients to attract genuine affection and new, passionate relationships.

Items Needed:

- 5 drops Cardamom Oil
- 6 drops Palmarosa Oil
- 6 drops Lemon Verbena
- 5 drops Rose Oil

This blend is meant to bring a new love into your life.

Fortune-Attracting Oil

Mix this good luck oil with aromatic herbs and essential oils to draw positive energies, turning everyday challenges into opportunities and attracting luck and prosperity.

Items Needed:

- 3 drops Vetivert Oil
- 2 drops Orange Oil
- 1 drop Clove Oil

To bring positive energies into your life.

Sensual Passion Oil

Blend this passion oil to ignite sensuality and desire, infusing it with alluring herbs and essential oils that awaken longing and deepen intimacy.

Items Needed:

- 5 drops Sandalwood Oil
- 3 drops Ylang-Ylang Oil
- 1 drops Orange Oil
- 2 drops Cinnamon Oil
- 2 drops Ginger Oil
- 2 drops Clove Oil

Note: These love spell oils can be used along with your favorite love spell or used on their own. They will have a powerful magick of their own but largely work better if prospective companions are able to smell them.

In other words, wearing love oil as you stay home and sit in your living room isn't going to be as effective as getting out around people.

Romantic Elixir Potion

Create this love potion with potent botanicals that captivate hearts, enhancing your magnetic aura and inviting deep connections with its irresistible blend.

What good is having a love spell without having a love potion? It's really a tea, but it smells great and it can help you relax and unwind, especially if you are too busy for love.

Items Needed:

- 2 tsp. Dried Jasmine Flowers
- 1 tbsp. Rose Petals
- 1 tsp. Dried Yerba Mate
- ¼ tsp. Vanilla Extract
- 2 Cinnamon Sticks
- 8 oz. Distilled or Spring Water
- Small Pot
- Cheesecloth

Directions:

Pour water into a pot. You can add more for a stronger potion or less for a weaker one. Add remaining ingredients to the water. Give the blend a little stir to combine everything, and then simmer for 3-5 minutes.

Remove from heat and strain immediately. Allow this to cool and then bottle it. Add mineral water. Can be served chilled or reheated.

Affection Soothing Bath

Indulge in this love bath to immerse yourself in an aromatic blend of herbs and oils that soothe the senses, cleanse your aura, and attract harmonious relationships.

Items Needed:

- 3 parts Rose Petals
- 2 parts Rose Geranium
- 1 part Ginger
- 1 part Cardamom
- Red Bag

Directions:

Mix the herbs in bowl visualizing your goal. When mixed, add about a handful or so into the sachet. Fill a clean tub with water. Place the sachet into the tub and let it steep until the water releases the energy, scents, and colors. If you prefer showers, use sachet as a scrub after you shower, but before you towel off. Place the unused portion in a jar with lid and store in dark cool place.

Passion Incense Blend

Craft this lovers' incense to kindle passion, combining fragrant herbs and resins that create an aromatic atmosphere to enhance intimacy, inspire desire, and attract harmonious romantic energy.

Items Needed

- 2 parts Sandalwood
- ½ part Basil
- ½ part Mint
- Drops of Rose Oil

Directions:

Mix dry ingredients together as you visualize on the incense's goal. Add in the oil. Once thoroughly mixed, empower the incense again. Burn on a charcoal disc. Place the unused portion in a jar with lid and store in dark cool place.

6

ENHANCING PERSONAL CHARISMA AND ATTRACTIVENESS

The concept of personal magick is an enchanting and empowering aspect of magical practice. It focuses on the individual's journey through self-discovery, enhancement, and transformation. Personal magick is essentially about harnessing one's inner energies and potential to effect a change in one's life and environment. This introductory exploration delves into what personal magick is, its foundational principles, and how individuals can practice it in their daily lives.

Understanding Personal Magick

Personal magick refers to the use of magical practices that focus specifically on the self. This can include spells, rituals, and techniques designed to enhance personal qualities, improve life circumstances, or manifest one's desires. Unlike other forms of magick that might concentrate on external influences or interceding on behalf of others, personal magick is introspective and deeply personal.

Foundational Principles

I. Intention

At the heart of personal magick is intention, the mental and emotional energy that one directs toward a desired outcome. Clear intentions are crucial to personal magick, as they guide the energies conjured and focused during any ritual or spell. Setting intentions involves deep self-reflection to truly understand one's desires and needs.

I. Energy Work

Energy is the currency of magick. Understanding and manipulating energies within and around oneself is essential. This can involve practices like meditation, chakra balancing, or the use of talismans or sigils that hold particular energies. Learning to sense and direct this energy is a skill developed over time and with practice.

I. Visualization

Visualization is a powerful tool of personal magick. It involves picturing the desired outcome in one's mind's eye as vividly and in as much detail as possible. This technique helps to focus the mind and direct energy towards manifesting these visualized goals.

I. Correspondences

Magick often involves the use of correspondences—objects, colors, symbols, and even times of day or phases of the moon—that are believed to have particular energies or significances. Using correspondences that align with one's personal intentions can amplify the effectiveness of a magical work.

Practices in Personal Magick

Engaging in personal magick can vary widely depending on one's interests, beliefs, and the traditions one follows. Here are a few practices that can be incorporated into daily life:

- **Daily Affirmations:** Using affirmations reinforces one's intentions and positively aligns one's mindset every day.
- **Journaling:** Keeping a magickal journal helps in tracking progress, growth, and the effectiveness of different practices.
- **Rituals:** Creating small, personal rituals that are performed consistently can strengthen one's magickal practice and create a rhythm in one's life.
- **Divination:** Techniques like tarot or rune casting can provide insights and guidance for personal growth and decision-making.

Starting Your Journey

For those new to personal magick, the key is to start small. Begin by spending time in meditation each day to connect with your inner self and your desires. Experiment with crafting small spells or charms that focus on clear, attainable goals. Education is also crucial; read widely about different magical systems and practices to find what resonates with you and your personal ethos.

Personal magick is a path of empowerment and self-discovery. It invites practitioners to look inward and harness their own power to influence their world. By understanding and applying its principles, anyone can unlock their potential and transform their life through magic. This journey into personal magick not only enhances one's life but also deepens one's connection to the universe and its myriad mysteries.

Charisma Enhancement Spells

Charisma enhancement spells are a fascinating aspect of magical practices aimed at amplifying one's personal allure and social influence. These spells are particularly sought after by individuals who wish to improve their interpersonal relationships, enhance their social presence, or boost their confidence in public or private settings. The philosophy behind these spells centers on the belief that everyone possesses an innate energy or aura that can be shaped and intensified to attract positive attention and admiration from others.

Understanding Charisma Enhancement Spells

Charisma, by definition, is an interesting attractiveness or charm that can inspire devotion in others. In magical terms, enhancing charisma involves amplifying these qualities through specific rituals and spells that align one's inner energy with the energies of attraction and confidence. This practice is not about deceiving or manipulating others, but enhancing one's natural qualities that foster positive interactions.

Critical Components of Charisma Enhancement Spells

I. Intention Setting

Like all magical practices, charisma enhancement spells begin with setting a clear and focused intention. Practitioners must identify what aspects of their charisma they wish to enhance— be it their ability to communicate, their confidence, or their general appeal—and hold this intention clearly in their minds throughout the ritual.

1. Use of Correspondences

Certain elements are believed to correspond with personal attraction and charisma. These often include:

- **Colors:** Red represents passion and confidence, yellow represents friendliness and approachability, and pink represents charm and sweetness.
- **Crystals:** Stones like rose quartz for love, tiger's eye for confidence, and citrine for charisma.
- **Herbs:** Basil is for love and protection, lavender is for calming and clarity, and cinnamon is for success and healing.
- **Days and Phases of the Moon:** Spells cast on a Friday (Venus's day, the planet of love) or during the waxing moon (when the moon grows fuller, symbolizing growth and accumulation) are believed to be more effective.

1. Visualization Techniques

Visualization is a powerful tool in charisma enhancement spells. Practitioners are encouraged to visualize themselves as being surrounded by a radiant light that attracts others to them. This visualization not only focuses the spell's energy but also psychologically prepares the practitioner to act with confidence and charm.

Sample Charisma Enhancement Spell

Here's a simple spell that one might perform to enhance personal charisma:

1. **Prepare Your Space:** Cleanse your space and yourself to remove any negative energy. This can be done with smoke from sage or incense.
2. **Gather Your Items:** Arrange the corresponding items around you. Light a pink candle for charm, hold a piece of rose quartz, and perhaps sprinkle some basil leaves.
3. **Set Your Intention:** Clearly state your intention. You might say something like, "I am radiant, charming, and confident. I attract kindness and positive attention wherever I go."
4. **Visualize:** Close your eyes and imagine a light emanating from within you, growing brighter and more interesting.
5. **Seal the Spell:** Conclude by saying, "So mote it be," or a similar phrase, signaling the completion of the spell. Allow the candle to burn down safely.

Ethical Considerations

It's essential to approach charisma enhancement spells with respect to free will and ethical considerations. The goal should not be to coerce or manipulate, but to enhance one's positive qualities that naturally draw others.

Charisma enhancement spells offer a spiritual tool for self-improvement, helping practitioners ethically boost their social skills and personal magnetism. By focusing on amplifying their best qualities, individuals can foster more meaningful and positive interactions in every area of their lives, reflecting the true essence of what it means to use magic responsibly.

Self-Love Spells

Self-love spells are an integral part of personal magick, aimed at nurturing one's own emotional well-being and self-acceptance. In a world where external pressures and self-doubt can quickly erode self-esteem, these spells offer a spiritual remedy to strengthen inner confidence and foster a deep-seated appreciation of oneself. The practice of self-love spells involves rituals and intentions focused on enhancing one's self-image, cultivating love within oneself, and promoting overall mental and emotional healing.

Understanding Self-Love Spells

Self-love spells are not about egoism or vanity. Instead, they are crafted to help individuals recognize their worth, heal from past traumas, and break free from the cycle of negative self-perception and critical self-talk. These spells work on the premise that by changing how we internally view ourselves, we can alter our external experiences and interactions for the better.

Critical Elements of Self-Love Spells

1. Cleansing and Preparation

The first step in any self-love spell involves cleansing oneself and one's environment to remove negative energies. This might include a bath with sea salt or herbal mixtures to purify the body and mind or smudging one's space with sage or Palo Santo.

1. Intention Setting

Clarity of intention is crucial in self-love spells. Practitioners should focus on specific aspects of self-love they wish to enhance, such as self-forgiveness, self-respect, or self-compassion. Articulating these intentions clearly helps to direct the spell's energy effectively.

1. Use of Correspondences

Certain items are believed to enhance self-love magick, including:

- **Crystals:** Rose quartz for unconditional love, amethyst for healing, and clear quartz for clarity.
- **Candles:** Pink for affection, green for healing, or white for purity.
- **Oils and Herbs:** Lavender for peace, chamomile for soothing, and cinnamon for success.
- **Symbols:** Symbols that represent love and positivity can also be incorporated, such as hearts or written affirmations.

1. Ritual Execution

Self-love spells often involve a ritual or ceremony. This might include lighting candles, arranging crystals, applying oils, and reciting affirmations or chants focused on loving oneself. The ritual should be performed in a quiet, comfortable space where the practitioner feels at ease.

Sample Self-Love Spell

Here's a basic self-love spell that can be easily performed:

1. **Prepare Your Space:** Ensure the area is clean and quiet. Light a pink candle and have rose quartz nearby.
2. **Bath Ritual:** Take a warm bath with salts and a few drops of lavender oil. As you soak, clear your mind and focus on feelings of love towards yourself.
3. **Affirmation and Visualization:** While drying off, recite affirmations that reinforce your worth and love for yourself. Visualize your body glowing with a bright, loving light.
4. **Seal the Spell:** Finish the ritual by anointing yourself with a self-love oil on your heart area and repeating, "I am worthy of love, I accept love, I give love freely to myself."

Ethical Considerations and Impact

Self-love spells are a purely positive practice with no ethical dilemmas, as they focus solely on the self and harm no one. The impact of these spells can be profoundly transformative, helping individuals to develop a more compassionate and forgiving relationship with themselves.

Self-love spells serve as powerful tools for those seeking to enhance their self-esteem and emotional well-being. By fostering a nurturing relationship with oneself, individuals are better equipped to face life's challenges through resilience and confidence. The practice encourages a holistic approach to healing, where the nurturing of the mind and spirit plays a critical role in personal development and happiness.

THE ETHICS OF LOVE MAGIC

Understanding the ethics in any field, particularly in practices involving influence and power such as magic, business, or technology, is critical for maintaining integrity, trust, and sustainability. Ethics serve as the moral framework from which individuals and societies gauge the rightness or wrongness of actions. They influence how we interact with others, the environment, and ourselves, providing a guide to conduct that upholds dignity and respect for all involved.

Foundation of Ethics

The foundation of ethics is built upon critical principles such as fairness, responsibility, honesty, and respect for others' rights and dignity. These principles help to ensure that actions and decisions do not harm others and that they promote the greater good. In contexts where power dynamics are significant, such as in magical practices or leadership roles, the necessity of ethical consideration is amplified because of the potential impact on individuals' lives and well-being.

Ethics in Magical Practices

Ethics primarily revolve around the concepts of consent, harm, and manipulation in magical practices. Because of their personal and often intimate nature, navigating ethics is delicate and essential.

Consent

Consent is a fundamental ethical principle in magic and any interaction involving two or more parties. It consists of gaining explicit permission from anyone directly affected by a spell or magical work. This principle is especially pertinent in love spells or any magic intended to alter someone's thoughts, feelings, or life circumstances. Performing magic without consent is viewed as manipulative and an infringement of another's free will.

Harm None

The Wiccan Rede, "An it harm none, do what ye will," encapsulates a widespread ethical stance in many magical traditions. This guideline advises practitioners to refrain from actions that could cause harm, whether physically, emotionally, or spiritually. It promotes the pursuit of personal goals and magical practices as long as they do not adversely affect others.

The Threefold Law

Also significant in magical ethics, particularly in Wicca and other neo-pagan traditions, is the Threefold Law. This law posits that whatever energy a person puts out into the world, whether positive or negative, will return to that person three times over. This concept encourages practitioners to consider the long-term effects of their actions, reinforcing the importance of positive practices.

Ethical Challenges and Considerations

Ethical challenges arise when the lines between influence and manipulation blur. For example, a spell to boost one's confidence or charisma is considered ethically sound, as it primarily affects the practitioner. However, a spell intended to make another person fall in love or act against their will crosses ethical boundaries. Such practices can lead to questions about the moral implications of interfering with another person's life path or personal choices.

Promoting Ethical Awareness

Promoting ethical awareness involves education and open discussion about the consequences of one's actions. It requires a critical examination of one's motives and the potential ripple effects of any action. In groups or communities where magical practices are shared, establishing clear ethical guidelines can help to cultivate a culture of respect and responsibility.

Understanding and adhering to ethical principles is crucial in maintaining the integrity and effectiveness of any practice, magical or otherwise. It ensures that practitioners operate not only for personal gain but also for the welfare of others, respecting individual autonomy and promoting mutual benefit. As society grows and alternative forms of influence emerge, the discussion and understanding of ethics must also adapt, ensuring that they continue to serve as a reliable guide for righteous conduct.

Consent in Magical Practices

Consent in magical practices is a foundational ethical principle that ensures respect for individual autonomy and freedom. In the realm of magic, particularly in practices that involve influencing others' thoughts, emotions, or circumstances, getting explicit consent is not just a courtesy; it's a moral imperative. This concept is crucial for maintaining integrity within the magical community and for upholding the dignity and rights of all individuals involved.

Understanding Consent in Magic

Consent in magic refers to the explicit approval given by individuals before any magical work is done that affects them directly or indirectly. This could range from healing spells to more complex rituals that might influence someone's personal or emotional state. The necessity for consent is based on the premise that every person has sovereign control over their own spiritual, emotional, and physical well-being.

Ethical Dimensions of Consent

Respect for Free Will: At the heart of the ethical practice of magic is the respect for free will. This principle asserts that individuals may decide about their lives without undue external influence. Performing magic on someone without their consent can be seen as an attempt to override this fundamental right, equating to spiritual or psychological coercion.

Avoiding Harm: The principle of "harm none," widely accepted in many magical traditions, is directly tied to the concept of consent. Casting spells without the informed consent of those involved can lead to unintended consequences that might harm the target or even create karmic repercussions for the practitioner. By ensuring consent, practitioners aim to prevent adverse outcomes and uphold the ethical integrity of their work.

Transparency and Honesty: Consent is only valid if it is informed. This means that the person giving consent should fully know the nature of the magical work, its intended effects, and any potential risks involved. Transparency and honesty from the practitioner are essential in ensuring that the consent given is genuinely informed and, thus, ethically sound.

Practical Considerations in Obtaining Consent

Communicating Effectively

Effective communication is key to obtaining consent. Practitioners must clearly explain the purpose, methods, and potential effects of the magical work they propose. This dialogue should be free of coercion, allowing the individual to make a voluntary and unpressured decision.

Consent in Group Settings

In group rituals or communal magical practices, getting consent from all participants is crucial. Each participant should agree to the specifics of the ritual, including any chants, movements, or the use of personal artifacts. Group leaders should facilitate an environment where individuals express concerns or opt-out without judgment.

Documenting Consent

Documenting consent might be advisable in more formal or intense magical practices. This could be as simple as a verbal agreement or as formal as a written consent form, especially in public or semi-public settings where the specifics of the ritual are complex or carry significant emotional or spiritual weight.

Challenges in Managing Consent

The challenge in managing consent in magical practices is ensuring that it is ongoing. Consent can be withdrawn, and practitioners must be prepared to halt or change their work accordingly. The subjective nature of many magical practices can make it difficult to fully articulate potential outcomes, requiring practitioners to operate with high sensitivity and adaptability.

Consent is a critical aspect of ethical magical practices, reflecting a deep respect for individual autonomy and practitioners' moral responsibilities. By prioritizing consent, the magical community upholds its integrity. It fosters a positive and respectful environment where the spiritual growth and personal boundaries of every individual are honored.

Responsible Spellcasting

Responsible spellcasting is an essential aspect of ethical magical practice, emphasizing the importance of accountability, consideration of consequences, and respect for both natural and spiritual laws. This concept encourages practitioners to engage in magic with mindfulness, ensuring that their actions align with ethical principles and contribute positively to their surroundings. Responsible spellcasting is crucial not only for the welfare of others but also for the integrity and personal growth of the practitioner.

Foundations of Responsible Spellcasting

1. Intentionality

At the core of responsible spellcasting lies the precise and deliberate setting of intentions. This involves deep self-reflection to understand the true motives behind a spell. Practitioners must ensure their intentions are not driven by impulsive desires, vengeance, or manipulative aims. By focusing on positive and self-improving intentions, spellcasters can avoid unintended harm and align their practices with the highest ethical standards.

1. Knowledge and Preparation

Responsible spellcasting requires a thorough understanding of the spells being cast, including the potential effects and the contexts for their use. This means practitioners should educate themselves on the different components of their spells, such as herbs, stones, symbols, and their associated energies. Preparation also involves understanding the historical and cultural contexts of specific practices to avoid cultural appropriation or misuse of traditional knowledge.

1. Consent and Impact on Others

Consent is paramount in responsible spellcasting. Practitioners must seek explicit permission from anyone directly affected by their spells. This respects the autonomy and free will of all individuals involved. Responsible spellcasters consider the broader impact of their actions, ensuring that their spells do not harm the community or environment or disrupt natural balance.

1. Ethical Guidelines

Adhering to ethical guidelines is a staple of responsible spellcasting. Many magical traditions offer specific ethical codes, such as the Wiccan Rede's "An it harm none, do what ye will" or the Threefold Law, which posits that whatever energy a spellcaster puts into the world will return threefold. These guidelines help practitioners to consider the long-term consequences of their actions, promoting a mindful and holistic approach to magic.

Practical Aspects of Responsible Spellcasting

Recording spells and their outcomes is a practical method for maintaining responsibility. It allows spellcasters to track their progress, learn from experiences, and adjust their practices to prevent negative consequences. Recording also fosters transparency and accountability within the magical community.

Environmental Considerations

Responsible spellcasting also involves environmental consciousness. Practitioners should source their materials ethically, use energy sparingly, and ensure that their spell remnants do not harm the environment. This respect for nature not only aligns with the ecological sensibilities of many magical practices, but also enhances the effectiveness and harmony of the spells cast.

Personal Accountability

Finally, responsible spellcasting demands personal accountability. Practitioners must own the outcomes of their spells, learning from both successes and mistakes. This accountability involves a willingness to rectify any harm caused and to adjust practices to prevent future issues.

Responsible spellcasting is a multifaceted approach that encompasses ethical, practical, and personal dimensions. By practicing spellcasting responsibly, practitioners not only safeguard the well-being of others and the environment, but also deepen their own magical practice and personal integrity. This approach ensures that magic remains a positive, transformative force aligned with both individual aspirations and the greater good.

CONCLUSION

As we draw to a close on our comprehensive exploration of love magic, it is crucial to pause and reflect on the fundamental aspects we've covered. The power of love magic surpasses simply casting spells to seek or protect romantic relationships. This mystical journey involves more than manipulating energies to achieve desired outcomes—it's about nurturing a deeper connection between oneself and the universe.

Integrating Love Magic into Daily Life

Incorporating love magic into your life should not be occasional. This integration means applying the principles of love magic in everyday interactions and decisions, infusing every action with intention and integrity. Love magic has the power to transform and enhance all aspects of your life, bringing hope and optimism.

Continuing Your Magical Practice

Love magic, like all forms of magic, is dynamic and ever-evolving. It grows with you and adapts to new insights and experiences. If you want to progress in your magical practice, you need to be fully dedicated to learning and personal growth. Actively engage with the magical community, participate in discussions, exchange experiences, and delve into the wealth of knowledge from both past and present practitioners. Keeping a magical journal is beneficial; it helps you document your spells, thoughts, and the lessons learned along the way, serving as a reflective tool and a personal guide.

Regular practice paired with reflection enhances not only your skill but also your spiritual depth. This journal will evolve into a valuable repository of personal wisdom, documenting your progress as both a professional and an individual. Be receptive to exploring various magical systems and traditions, which refer to different approaches and methods of practicing magic. Your practice is enriched by this openness, giving you a broader framework to gain wisdom from.

Sustaining Growth and Ethical Practice

To assure the continual growth of magic, it is important to maintain ethical standards that value the free will and dignity of all beings. The magic you cast should always consider the potential impact on others and the world. Engage in practices that promote positive energy and constructive outcomes, and steer clear of actions that could cause harm or manipulate others. This responsibility and consideration are integral to the practice of love magic.

Keep in mind, in love magic, the real power comes from the personal growth that the spells initiate, not from the spells themselves. Each spell is an opportunity for personal reflection, growth, and a deeper connection with the broader universe. Embrace this journey with an open heart and a clear conscience, guided by the principles of love, respect, and wisdom.

As you journey forward, may the magic you possess bring light to your life and the lives of those around you. Love magic is ultimately about the power to change, to heal, and to brighten the world—one spell at a time. It's a tribute to the meaningful bonds in life and a testament to the transformative power of conscientious, enchanting rituals on the world. For instance, a thoughtful, ethical, magical practice could involve casting a spell to promote harmony in a relationship rather than to control or manipulate the other person. Allow this to guide you as you delve into the magical realm of love, forging connections that are fulfilling and transformative.

REFERENCES

Spell Jars: Magic In A Bottle » Grandma's Grimoire. https://grandmasgrimoire.com/spell-jars-magic-in-a-bottle/

Discover the Best self esteem Books in the 2024 Updated Edition. https://edgemontlibrary.org/discover-the-best-self-esteem-books-in-the-2024-updated-edition/

Wiccan Beliefs & Practices For Beginners- What Do Wiccans Do? – Curious Cauldron. https://curiouscauldron.com.au/blogs/sacred-space/wiccan-beliefs-and-practices-for-beginners

Law of Reincarnation Raw - The Ice Creamists. https://www.theicecreamists.com/law-of-reincarnation-raw

Self love and Mental Health. https://www.mayahslegacy.com/post/self-love-and-mental-health

ABOUT THE AUTHOR

Monique Joiner Siedlak is a writer, witch, and warrior on a mission to awaken people to their greatest potential through the power of storytelling infused with mysticism, modern paganism, and new age spirituality. At the young age of 12, she began rigorously studying the fascinating philosophy of Wicca. By the time she was 20, she was self-initiated into the craft, and hasn't looked back ever since. To this day, she has authored over 40 books pertaining to the magick and mysteries of life.

To find out more about Monique Joiner Siedlak artistically, spiritually, and personally, feel free to visit her **official website**.

www.mojosiedlak.com

facebook.com/mojosiedlak

x.com/mojosiedlak

instagram.com/mojosiedlak

pinterest.com/mojosiedlak

bookbub.com/authors/monique-joiner-siedlak

MORE BOOKS BY MONIQUE

African Spirituality Beliefs and Practices

Hoodoo

Seven African Powers: The Orishas

Cooking for the Orishas

Lucumi: The Ways of Santeria

Voodoo of Louisiana

Haitian Vodou

Orishas of Trinidad

Connecting with your Ancestors

Blood Magick

The Orishas

Vodun: West Africa's Spiritual Life

Marie Laveau: Life of a Voodoo Queen

Candomblé: Dancing for the God

Umbanda

Exploring the Rich and Diverse World

Divination Magic for Beginners

Divination with Runes

Divination with Diloggún

Divination with Osteomancy

Divination with the Tarot

Divination with Stones

The Beginner's Guide to Inner Growth

Astral Projection for Beginners

Meditation for Beginners

Reiki for Beginners

Mastering Your Inner Potential

Creative Visualization

Manifesting With the Law of Attraction

Holistic Healing and Energy

Healing Animals with Reiki

Crystal Healing

Communicating with Your Spirit Guides

Empathic Understanding and Enlightenment

Being an Empath Today

Life on Fire

Healing Your Inner Child

Change Your Life

Raising Your Vibe

The Indie Author's Guides

The Indie Author's Guide to Fast Drafting Your Novel

Get a Handle on Life

Get a Handle on Stress

Time Bound

Get a Handle on Anxiety

Get a Handle on Depression

Get a Handle on Procrastination

The Holistic Yoga and Wellness Series

Yoga for Beginners

Yoga for Stress

Yoga for Back Pain

Yoga for Weight Loss

Yoga for Flexibility

Yoga for Advanced Beginners

Yoga for Fitness

Yoga for Runners

Yoga for Energy

Yoga for Your Sex Life

Yoga to Beat Depression and Anxiety

Yoga for Menstruation

Yoga to Detox Your Body

Yoga to Tone Your Body

The DIY Body Care Series

Creating Your Own Body Butter

Creating Your Own Body Scrub

Creating Your Own Body Spray

WANT TO BE
FIRST TO KNOW?

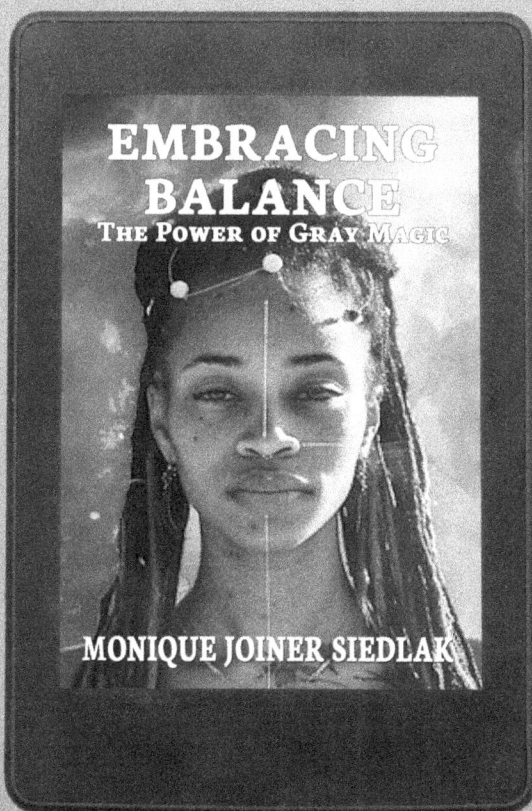

EMBRACING
BALANCE
The Power of Gray Magic

MONIQUE JOINER SIEDLAK

JOIN MY NEWSLETTER!
WWW.MOJOSIEDLAK.COM/MOONLIGHT-MUSINGS

SUPPORT ME BY
LEAVING A REVIEW!

goodreads

amazon

BookBub

Download on
Apple Books

GET IT ON
Google Play

nook
by Barnes & Noble

Rakuten
kobo

www.ingramcontent.com/pod-product-compliance
Lightning Source LLC
Chambersburg PA
CBHW071612040426
42452CB00008B/1317